RHINOS IN NEBRASKA

THE AMAZING DISCOVERY OF THE ASHFALL FOSSIL BEDS

RHINOS IN NEBRASKA

THE AMAZING DISCOVERY
OF THE ASHFALL FOSSIL BEDS

ALISON PEARCE STEVENS

ILLUSTRATED BY MATT HUYNH

HENRY HOLT AND COMPANY

NEW YORK

Henry Holt and Company, *Publishers since 1866*
Henry Holt® is a registered trademark of Macmillan Publishing Group, LLC
120 Broadway, New York, NY 10271 • mackids.com

Library of Congress Control Number: 2020040799

Our books may be purchased in bulk for promotional, educational, or business use.
Please contact your local bookseller or the Macmillan Corporate and
Premium Sales Department at (800) 221-7945 ext. 5442 or by
email at MacmillanSpecialMarkets@macmillan.com.

First edition, 2021 / Designed by Liz Dresner
Printed in the United States of America by
LSC Communications, Harrisonburg, Virginia

ISBN 978-1-250-26657-6

1   3   5   7   9   10   8   6   4   2

*For everyone who seeks to
uncover Earth's mysteries*

TABLE OF CONTENTS

GLIMPSE OF AN ANCIENT PAST

Picture this: a vast grassy plain, dotted here and there with trees. A small herd of rhinos thunders by. An elephant trumpets in the distance. A long, giraffe-like neck stretches into the branches of a tree. A herd of grazing mammals—are those zebras?—lift their heads, all of them suddenly nervous. And no wonder. An animal that looks a bit like a hyena rustles the grass nearby.

Where is this exotic location?

It must be Africa.

Or is it?

Take a closer look at those animals. The rhinos are definitely rhinos. But with their short, squatty legs and round bodies, they look a bit like hippos.

The elephant, when it lifts its trunk, shows off *four* tusks, not two. That giraffe, on closer inspection, actually looks kind of like a camel.

And the zebras turn out to be several different kinds of horses. Some are zebra-sized, others the size of small ponies. They all have hooves, but some have three on each foot!

The hyena? Although it has similarly powerful, bone-crushing jaws, this animal is something else entirely. Hyenas aren't dogs, but this animal is. And—whoa! The deer that just bounded by had three horns.

Do you know where you are now?

No?

Would you believe it's the middle of North America?

Welcome to Nebraska . . . twelve million years ago.

How do we know that ancient Nebraska used to look like today's African **savanna**? Through the hard work of many scientists and one extraordinary discovery.

But before we get to that, let's go back to that grassland.

There's a **water hole** nearby. It's not a proper lake or pond, because it isn't always there. When rain falls, it fills. Animals come by to drink. But when the dry season comes, the water slowly evaporates. It soaks into the ground. After a while, the water hole is nothing more than mud.

Seasons here—both on the African savanna and in ancient Nebraska—aren't determined by warm temperatures versus cold ones. Temps stay mild (above freezing) all year long. Instead, seasons are defined by rainfall, creating a wet season and a dry one. During the dry season, the water hole is an important source of water for the animals that live here. Even those that don't live nearby will travel a long way to visit.

What critters might have come to this ancient place to drink? Rhinos, elephants, horses, and camels of many kinds. Predators, including several kinds of wild dogs, a saber-toothed "cat," and a **beardog** that's neither bear nor dog.

A strange creature called an **oreodont**.

Deer with three horns or saber teeth. Horned rodents. Birds, turtles, snakes, and more.

Now imagine it's an ordinary day for these animals. They're doing what animals do—eating, drinking, and trying not to become someone else's lunch. It's that time of year when there are lots of mothers with their babies.

Seems peaceful, doesn't it?

But a thousand miles away, trouble is brewing. These animals don't know it, but everything is about to change.

SUPERVOLCANO

L et's hop to the west, into what we now call Idaho. Deep beneath the earth's surface lies a massive chamber. It has been filling with hot molten **magma** for thousands of years. The superheated rock churns beneath the surface, pressing against the walls of the chamber. The pressure triggers a swarm of earthquakes. The ground shakes again and again as the magma pushes against the underside of the earth's surface. It pushes *pushes* PUSHES until . . . *KABOOM*!

The volcano explodes. But this is no ordinary volcano; it's a **supervolcano**. Rock, ash, and lava shoot into the sky from one part of the enormous volcano after another. The sky turns dark. There is so much power behind the eruption that rock and ash reach high into the **atmosphere** before they start raining down again. The area near the super-volcano is obliterated.

Strong winds carry the chunks of rock and ash east. As they go, they continue to fall from the sky, blanketing everything in their path. Bigger pieces fall out sooner, bombarding the ground, burying everything in more than two feet of debris. Lighter ash stays airborne longer, riding the wind current as it travels across the continent. Ash settles out over days and weeks. The wind carries some ash all the way to the Atlantic Ocean, more than two thousand miles away.

Many times larger than the 1980 eruption of Mount
St. Helens (depicted in the upper left corner), the
supervolcano's ash traveled across the entire continent.

Back at the water hole in the ancient savanna, a cloud
of ash appears on the horizon. It may have looked like any
other storm when it first appeared, but the animals soon
found themselves surrounded by fluffy, gray flakes.

Ash was everywhere. The animals breathed it in. It covered the ground and settled into the water hole. For many of
these animals, the ash was a death sentence. Birds, turtles,
and other small animals died almost immediately, their sensitive lungs easily damaged. Larger animals—deer, horses,

and camels—lasted longer, days or perhaps a few weeks. And the biggest—the rhinos—lasted a month or more before the ash did them in.

But how do we know all this? It happened twelve million years ago. No one was there with a video camera or a notebook. In fact, no people existed at all. How can we possibly know what happened to the animals at *this* water hole at *that* time?

Welcome to the Ashfall Fossil Beds. They hold the secret of this ancient past. For fifty years, scientists have been uncovering information about what happened in Nebraska during that eruption. They have pieced together a detailed picture of ancient life.

Let's find out how they did it.

UNUSUAL FIND

We're back in modern times. The water hole holds water no longer—it hasn't done so for millions of years. It filled with ash, which was then covered by sand and other **sediment**. Time passed, turning the sand into sandstone. Plants grew over the hillside. It looked like any other location in the rolling hills of northern Nebraska, but for one curious thing: Farmers who lived in this area frequently found bones in the gully. In fact, it happened so often, people called it Bone Hill.

People thought the bones were from cattle that had wandered into the area and died. They were about the right size, and there were plenty of cattle around at the time. But one day, a local father and son realized they'd found something more.

Donald Peterson was seventeen when the farmer who owned the land around Bone Hill hired Donald and his dad, James, to plant rye in the fields nearby. During a break they searched for "relics" (arrowheads, fossils, and petrified wood). Fossils have always been abundant in Nebraska. The state is one of the best places in the world to find fossils of ancient land **mammals**.

On this particular day, Donald and James checked out the gully at the base of Bone Hill. They clambered up the steep cliff and spotted something rough poking out from the chalk-like earth. Clinging to their precarious spot at the top of the cliff, they discovered teeth—teeth still sitting in a jaw that was attached to the rest of a skull.

The skull was eroding out of the hillside, where a recent rain had washed away the surrounding earth. Donald and his dad chipped at the soft soil that held the bone in place. They knew it couldn't be a cow. Not when it was jutting from the side of a cliff, buried under several feet of rock and soil.

It was a remarkable find.

Most fossils are just bits and pieces: a single tooth, some shards of bone, a broken skull. When most animals die, their bodies are **scavenged** (eaten) before they can be buried in sand or silt. Bones get broken up. Some get washed away in a flood. Most simply **decompose**. Only a few wind up in places where they are buried and begin the process of becoming fossils.

That process is long and slow, as the bones and teeth

are slowly, *slowly*, *s-l-o-w-l-y* replaced with bits of mineral. Those minerals come from water that soaks into the ground around the buried bones. It even soaks into the bones themselves. Minerals move into the bones and teeth, eventually filling the openings and sometimes replacing the original parts with something that's almost rock-like.

It's rare for fossil hunters to find an intact skull. Skulls have thin bones that break easily, so they seldom survive long enough to fossilize. Even more unusual: The bones of this new skull were not completely mineralized, like most fossils. They still had much of their bony structure. That's why Bone Hill seemed to be the place where cattle went to die. What looked like ordinary cow bones were actually from ancient animals. Because the bones didn't look like fossils, people hadn't recognized them for what they were.

Donald and James stopped digging and called the University of Nebraska State Museum (UNSM). Two paleontologists, Lloyd Tanner and Henry Reider, headed north from

Lincoln, more than three hours away. When they saw the skull, they immediately identified it as a rhinoceros. Rhinos haven't lived in Nebraska for five million years, but they once ran in vast herds across the Great Plains of North America.

The scientists dug the skull out of the ground, encasing it in plaster to protect it. They also took detailed field notes about where it had been found. All paleontologists do this. Those notes are just as important as the fossil itself when researchers dig into an animal's past. The notes are kept in the research collections along with the fossils for future study.

The most important thing a field note should have is the exact spot where the fossil was found. Future researchers may need to revisit a site, and this helps them find it again. Simply saying it's a short hike from a nearby road won't do. Roads change over time, rivers cut new channels, and even hilltops can vanish under the quick work of a bulldozer. Recording the location with the **coordinates** for **latitude** and **longitude** works best. Those are easy for paleontologists to get now, since every smartphone has built-in **GPS** (Global Positioning System).

Back in 1953, when the rhino skull was found, the paleontologists were a bit less specific with their locations. They had to be—GPS hadn't been invented yet! But they did have photos taken from an airplane that had flown over the area. This aerial image gave them a bird's-eye view of the land. A few years later, a better tool became available: a **topographic map**. These maps (sometimes called "topo maps")

show the lay of the land. Lines on the map represent different heights or elevations.

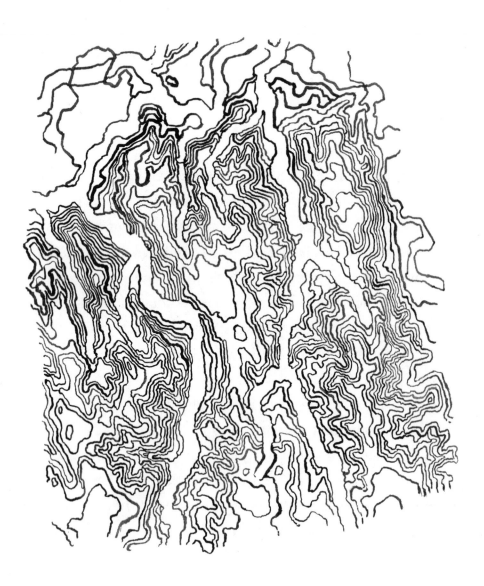

A topographic map.

Imagine placing a large bowl upside down and running a marker around the outside of it. You could do this around the base, again one inch up, then another inch up, and so on until you reach the top. If you look down on the bowl from the top, you will see circles inside of circles. Each one represents one specific height on the outside of the bowl. You could draw those circles on a piece of paper, and the result would be a topographic map of the bowl.

In the same way, geologists draw hills and valleys on topo maps. Those lines aren't perfect circles, like your bowl. Rather, they wiggle and wander, following the natural landscape.

Field notes also include sketches of the area, along with notes about them. Those can include call-outs (A patch of trees! A car-sized boulder!), or more descriptive text. All of this is to help that researcher—or other researchers—locate the spot if they need to come back. It also helps scientists who are working in the lab know where a **specimen** (fancy name for the item they found) turned up.

The paleontologists took the skull and their notes back to the museum. In a bizarre turn of events, no one saw that remarkable skull again for more than thirty years. And the field notes? At some point in time, they mysteriously vanished.

HITTING PAYDIRT

Fast-forward eighteen years. Two young **geologists**, Mike and Jane Voorhies, are in the area. They're mapping the different kinds of rocks and soils found there. Such maps are useful both for **paleontology** purposes (such as finding good places to search for fossils) and for helping people decide how land would best be used. After all, you wouldn't want to build a skyscraper on shifting sand!

Jane and Mike began to explore the area around Bone Hill. Jane quickly discovered it was covered with poison ivy. Already beginning to itch, she left Mike to explore on his own, since poison ivy didn't bother him.

As Mike worked his way along the gully next to Bone Hill, he, too, spotted something unusual in the chalky cliff.

He, Jane, and other geologists had found a layer of light gray ash in cliffs across northern Nebraska. The ash layer was normally one to two feet thick. But here it looked like it was seven or eight feet.

Mike clambered up to the top of the ash layer, pulled out a tape measure, and was shocked to find a full ten feet of ash. There was clearly something different about this location, and Mike knew he should collect some samples so he could learn more.

Scientists can date ash, or find out how old it is. They do this by studying crystals within the ash. Some types of crystals contain **radioactive** elements. These elements break down over time, through the process of **radioactive decay**. When that happens, they change from one element to another. For example, potassium to argon or uranium to lead. How fast they decay varies from one type to the next. But for each element, the rate of decay (how fast it happens) is always constant. In fact, it's so predictable, you could say it's like clockwork.

A few years before Mike discovered the thick layer of ash, scientists had figured out how to test crystals to determine their age. So Mike began to search for some. He dug near the bottom of the ash layer, searching for the biggest chunks, which would have fallen from the sky faster and settled at the bottom.

He didn't find any crystals. But when he looked up, he spotted a bone.

He pulled out a brush and dusted away the pale gray ash to reveal a jawbone complete with teeth. He recognized it as a baby rhino. It was in incredibly good condition.

The original baby rhino jawbone as Mike Voorhies found it. [Mike Voorhies]

Excited, Mike returned the next day to collect the jaw. He scraped away the soft ash and soon uncovered the entire skull. Mike wrapped it in plaster and removed it. That's when he spotted another bone—one of the rhino's neck **vertebrae** (the bones of the backbone). At that point, Mike wondered whether he might have found an entire skeleton. But he didn't have the time, tools, or helpers to find out. So he left.

He didn't return for another six years.

When Mike came back, he brought a small team of

paleontologists to help him work. (Jane was not one of them; she avoided the area, which Mike had named Poison Ivy Quarry.) The team began by looking for the rest of the baby rhino Mike had unearthed years before. Sure enough, the entire skeleton was there, from the neck to the tail and the tips of its toes (the skull, however, was already at the museum). Incredibly, the skeleton wasn't broken apart, like most fossils. Each bone was in place, exactly as it had been in life. They weren't even squashed or flattened.

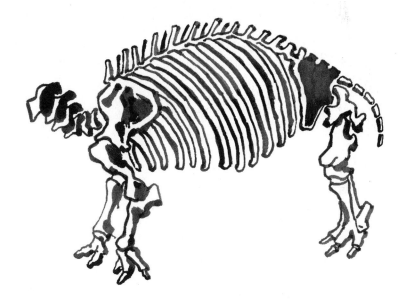

The scientists dug around the skeleton, wrapping it—and a good bit of ash—in a plaster jacket. It took four people to carry the weighty specimen to a pickup truck to take it back to the research collections in Lincoln.

The complete skeleton was an extraordinary discovery. But it wasn't the only one. As the team worked to free the baby rhino from the ash, their tools kept clicking against other hard objects. More bones, each one part of yet another skeleton. The researchers couldn't believe what they were uncovering. Nothing quite like it had been found anywhere else.

The team worked furiously to collect as many specimens as possible in the few weeks they had to work. They transported the skeletons of a dozen rhinos and three horses to the museum. They knew it was only a small amount of what was truly there. But to fully **excavate** the area, they would need to remove more than ten feet of sand, soil, and rock that sat atop the ash bed. That meant bringing in a bulldozer.

It was another year before the big equipment really opened things up for Mike and his team.

HOW OLD?

Paleontology is seasonal. Digging for fossils is possible only in good weather, so it happens over the summer. That winter, after the first dig, Mike and the museum staff studied the skeletons they had removed. Mike had lots of questions, but two loomed especially large: How old were the fossils at Poison Ivy Quarry? And where had all that ash come from, anyway?

Although Mike had looked for crystals, he hadn't found any during his exploration. That meant he couldn't have them dated. But he did know that barrel-bodied rhinos were common in Nebraska about ten million years ago. How, though, to find out if that was the actual time of the eruption that had killed these animals?

Mike puzzled about this. One day, he ran into John Boell-storff. John was an old friend from Mike's college days. At this point, John was working for the Nebraska Geological Survey.

And he happened to specialize in volcanic ash.

Mike told him about his discovery out at the quarry. To his surprise, John knew the spot. He had sampled some of that very ash, trying to figure out how it fit into all of the other ashfalls that had happened across the state over time.

John had discovered that there had been not one, but many volcanic eruptions and ashfall events over the millions of years of Nebraska's history. He had collected samples from each of these sites and brought them back to his lab. There, he put them in acid for a few minutes. Then he dried them off and examined them under a microscope. He scanned across each ash sample, carefully looking for—and recording—**fission** tracks.

Fission is what happens when a radioactive atom splits. It isn't a gentle process. When the atom breaks, it does so with a miniature explosion, rocketing minuscule pieces out from the middle. The movement is so powerful it leaves a tiny track behind (*really* tiny—remember that we're talking about something smaller than an atom!). The acid John used made these tracks a little bit bigger—big enough that he could see them under the microscope. He counted them up on slide after slide.

The longer ash has been sitting, the more times the

radioactive atoms inside have split. Brand-new ash has no fission tracks. Ash that's really ancient will have *lots*, simply because it's been around so long. By counting up the number of tracks in his samples, John could get an idea of how old the ash was.

He went to check his data and came back to Mike with a number: around 10.5 million years, plus or minus 1.5 million. Radioactive dating can't give us exact numbers. Instead it gives us a range of dates. Scientists know that their rock or fossil was created somewhere in that range. So the rhinos had died somewhere between twelve million and nine million years ago.

As for where the ash had come from, Mike had no idea. Neither did John. Mike knew of some volcanoes that had been active in New Mexico ten million years ago. He figured that must have been the source of the Poison Ivy Quarry ash.

It was the best he could do at the time with the information he had available.

HIDDEN IN ASH

The next summer, the paleontology team got serious. With the help of the bulldozer, they scraped off the rock and soil over an area about the size of a basketball court. Since they had found skeletons only in the bottom layers of ash, the team carefully bulldozed the top five feet of ash, as well. That left several feet of soft ash covering the fossils. It was enough that the heavy equipment couldn't damage the delicate specimens underneath, yet close enough that the scientists could dig down to the bones with ease.

The team then dug a grid of trenches across the exposed area. Some revealed fossils. Others didn't. Once the team knew the best places to start digging, they began clearing ash out of the grid, square by square.

They worked quickly at first, removing ash by the shovelful, filling buckets and hauling them into a nearby gully to dump. Putting it there helped them avoid breathing in the loose ash when the wind kicked up. An ash storm had killed the animals whose skeletons now lay just out of reach. The last thing the researchers needed were ash-related health problems of their own!

Volcanic ash is nothing like wood ash. Wood is mostly made of **carbon**, but it contains small amounts of minerals as well. These don't burn when the rest of the wood goes up in smoke. Instead, they're left behind as ash. These fluffy bits can be used as fertilizer. Breathing it in will make you cough, and a lot of it could gum up your lungs. But it generally won't cause severe damage.

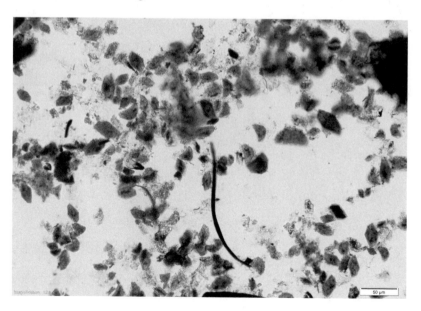

A magnified view of wood ash. [University of Nebraska State Museum]

Volcanic ash, on the other hand, is made up of tiny shards of glass. Their jagged edges and sharp points slice through delicate tissues of the body. And there's no tissue more delicate than the lungs. When it's breathed in, volcanic ash can do major damage to the lungs. Over time, unable to get enough air, animals begin to suffocate.

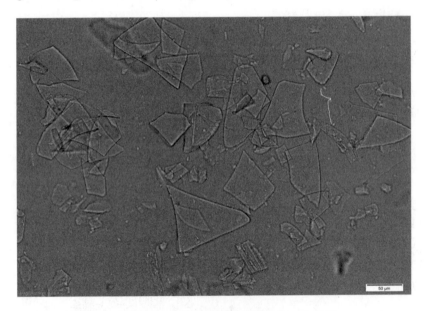

A magnified view of Ashfall's volcanic ash.
[University of Nebraska State Museum]

So it was important for the scientists to avoid inhaling the soft ash. Not an easy task, since there was so much of it!

When the wind kicked up, the researchers donned goggles and pulled masks over their noses and mouths. They coughed. The ash landed on their skin, its sharp edges digging in like tiny daggers, giving them a sense of what the animals had gone through so very long ago. The paleontologists crouched awkwardly, trying not to step on one skeleton while digging up another.

Paleontological digs always require a lot of hard work, but this site seemed to get more challenging every day. On the flip side, it was the discovery of a lifetime. The fossils were so abundant, in such good condition, and so easy to free from the ash that no one was willing to walk away.

The scientists worked from sunup to sundown every day for four months straight. By the time they were done, they had uncovered, jacketed (wrapped in plaster), and removed another fifty-eight rhinos. Five were adult males. The others were females and their one-, two-, and three-year-old young.

Preparing a jacket involves wrapping a fossil
in plaster. [Alison Pearce Stevens]

How did the researchers know the young rhinos' ages? They couldn't very well ask them. But they could (and did) check their teeth.

Just like you, young mammals, including rhinos, have baby teeth (also called milk teeth). They have just three on each side when they're first born. New ones come in as they get older. Looking into each rhino's mouth, scientists could see how many teeth had come in. This let them figure out how old the young rhinos were. They also knew the volcanic eruption had happened around the time of year when baby rhinos were born, because a few female skeletons had skeletons of their unborn young still nestled inside.

DEDUCING BEHAVIOR

The large numbers of females with their young suggested something else to Mike and his team: Unlike modern rhinos, barrel-bodied rhinos lived in herds.

It's not easy to learn about the behavior of extinct animals. After all, behavior is all about what an animal *does*. When we can't see animals doing what they do, it's challenging to say much about how they behaved when they were alive.

Scientists can make educated guesses based on how fossil bones and teeth are similar to those of living animals. That's actually one of the tools paleontologists use to understand new animals they unearth.

For example, researchers know that the thin-sabered "cat" *Barbourofelis* (BAR-bohr-oh-FEE-lis) was probably an ambush predator. (This predator lived at the time of the supervolcanic eruption. Scientists have found bones near the ash bed.) It waited for prey to wander by, then pounced on it. Scientists think this because of the animal's leg bones, which are short and stout, like those of a jaguar. Jaguars are sneaky, lying in wait for a tasty snack to wander by. Their legs are powerfully built for leaping and pouncing. The similarity between *Barbourofelis* bones and jaguar bones tells us the ancient animals probably hunted in a similar way.

Barbourofelis, a thin-sabered "cat" that researchers believe was an ambush predator.

How can scientists be sure? They have two more pieces of evidence.

First, *Barbourofelis* had super-long (seven-inch!), thin **canines** that could have easily broken in a struggle. Surprising their prey made it less likely their precious fangs would be damaged in a fight. Second, researchers compared the extinct animal's bones with those of animals that *do* chase down prey. The leg bones of cheetahs and wolves are long and thin, nothing like those of jaguars or *Barbourofelis*. So researchers can say with confidence that the thin-sabered "cat" was an ambush predator. (Why is "cat" in quotation marks? Because *Barbourofelis* wasn't a true cat. Although it looked similar to large cats, there are some important differences that tell us it was something else.)

Although bones and teeth can provide hints about an animal's behavior, they can only tell us so much. You can't say anything about how social animals were, for example— whether they hung out in groups or spent most of their time by themselves. For that, you need a whole collection of fossils that died together and were preserved in place. Luckily, that's exactly what Mike and his team had uncovered.

It was entirely possible that individual rhinos or mothers with their young had simply come to the water hole to drink. The large number of rhinos gathered in one place didn't necessarily mean they lived in herds. But Mike and his team thought they probably did. How did they know? Once again, they pieced together the animals' behavior by examining the evidence.

The rhinos were all found in a single layer of the ash. If individual animals had visited the water hole over time and died there, their bodies would have been at different heights in the ash. The fact that all seventy rhinos were found in one layer meant they had died within days of one another. So they probably lived in groups and traveled together.

The team also found that for every adult male, there were at least six adult females. Once again, the researchers turned to modern animals to understand this. In some modern herd animals, such as zebra and elk, females group together, and males defend one group from other males. In this way, the male can be sure he is the father of all young born into the group.

But keeping control of the group is hard work for these males. Males defending a group of females are always on alert. They need to be. Other males—those without mates— try again and again to take over the group. The male must defend his position over and over and over, sometimes in knock-down, drag-out fights. Males get injured. Bones can break.

The barrel-bodied rhinos fit the pattern seen in these modern animals. Bigger males almost always win, so younger, smaller males wouldn't have been able to defeat a powerful older male. Indeed, the team found only older, larger males in the ash. That, together with the large number of females and their young, suggests a similar kind of social structure.

What about the injuries that happen during combat? Several males had ribs that had healed from being broken in previous years. Rhinos often charge at each other, and broken ribs could have happened when one male rammed into another.

There's one final piece of evidence: In modern animals that have this social structure, young males form their own groups, called bachelor herds. Another paleontologist, Morris Skinner, had discovered fossils of a barrel-bodied rhino bachelor herd—nothing but young adult males—in a nearby location.

Even though the rhinos had been dead for millions of years, the paleontologists were able to add up all these pieces of information, compare what they found with what they knew about living animals, and come to a conclusion about the behavior of long-extinct rhinos.

Detective work at its finest.

A LONG, SLOW DEATH

Removing the rhino skeletons was difficult work. That was partly due to their massive size. Each skeleton plus the ash that cushioned it weighed up to a ton—as much as a small car! So the paleontologists had no choice but to remove each skeleton in sections. They jacketed legs separately from the rest of the body, for example. The pelvis was removed in one cast and the rib cage in another. The skulls were separated, too.

But even that wasn't easy.

The rhinos were so close to each other, it was nearly impossible not to step on one set of bones while trying to remove another. To make matters worse, those bones were extraordinarily delicate.

Even though bone seems solid, it actually has lots of little spaces in it. When most fossils form, those openings—and the bone itself—fill in with minerals that make them extremely tough. But the ash that buried the animals also locked them away from water. Since water couldn't flow past the bones in Poison Ivy Quarry, they didn't mineralize much. Millions of years later, they still had most of those gaps with just a few minerals here and there to hold it all together.

That wasn't the only problem. The bones had frothy bumps on the outside—spongy-looking bits of bone that had grown during the rhinos' last weeks of life. The paleontologists had to work carefully to avoid damaging the delicate fossils. One slip of a foot or tool could knock the strange growth off the bones. This revealed healthy bone underneath, but it removed vital evidence about what had happened to the animals.

The frothy bone is a sign of illness. Called Marie's disease, it's named after Pierre Marie, a French doctor who discovered it in 1890. Many animals, including people, can get Marie's disease. It's especially common when they can't breathe well. This could be due to injured lungs or an infection, such as pneumonia. In the case of the rhinos, it was caused when the ash damaged their lungs.

When an animal can't breathe well, the body responds—for reasons scientists still don't really understand—by making new, frothy growth on the bones. This starts in the hands and feet and spreads onto the long bones of the arms and legs. The growth causes swelling and stiffness, making it hard to move. It causes a fever, too.

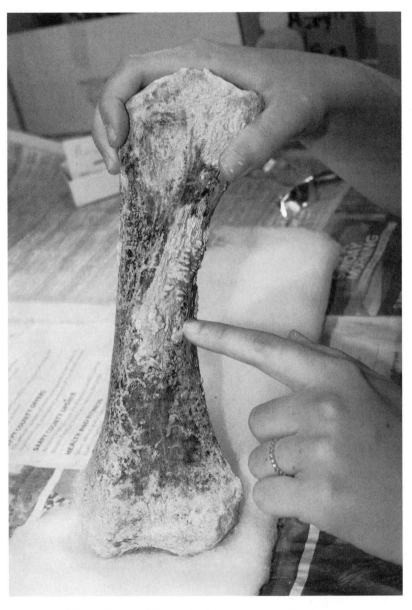

The white sections of this bone are the frothy growth of Marie's disease. [Alison Pearce Stevens]

Marie's disease shows up only in animals or people that have trouble breathing for a long time. That's because bone grows slowly. (If you've ever broken a bone, you know how long it takes to heal!) The thick layers of Marie's disease on the rhino bones told the researchers that the rhinos hadn't died a quick death. They weren't simply buried by the original ashfall. The ash *did* kill them, but it took a long time— several weeks, maybe longer.

Why would it have taken so long? One reason is their large lungs. Bigger animals have bigger lungs, which makes sense if you think about having to fit those branching, balloon-like organs inside a rib cage. They also breathe much more slowly than smaller animals do. It takes several seconds to fill those sizable air sacs. And then several seconds more to breathe it all out again.

Really big animals, like Asian elephants, breathe only four or five times a minute. Small songbirds, with their small lungs, breathe more than one hundred times per minute. The smallest mammal—the itty-bitty Etruscan shrew, which weighs about as much as four paper clips—breathes more than 650 times a minute. And that's when it's resting! Modern rhinos breathe about nineteen times per minute. So it would have taken the ancient rhinos a long time to breathe in the ash from the air. Little by little, it both filled up and sliced up their lungs.

SOLVING OLD MYSTERIES

Poison Ivy Quarry held a treasure trove of rhinos. That was clearly the case the first year, when Mike and his team had found lots of rhinos with a couple of horses mixed in. It appeared to be the case during the start of the second season as well.

But as the team dug deeper, they uncovered a much bigger story.

As they removed the rhinos, the more delicate skeletons of horses and camels came into view. Unlike the rhinos, which all belonged to the same species, five kinds of horses and three different camels were unearthed. The horses were especially interesting—and they helped solve some old mysteries.

New Skeleton
Discovered
July 22, 2017

Large 3-toed Horse
Neohipparion affine

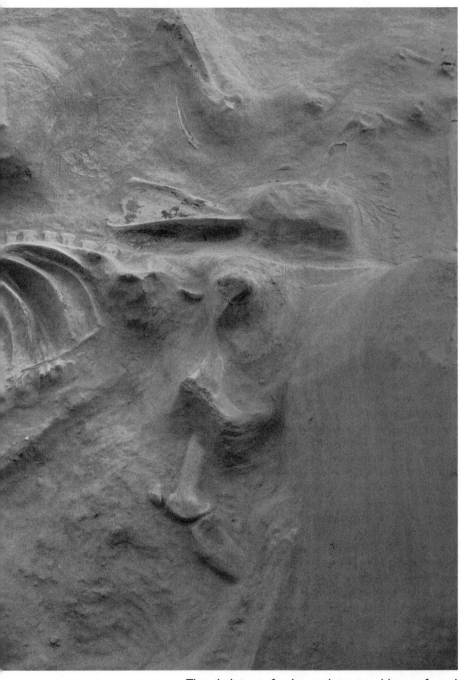

The skeleton of a large three-toed horse found
at Ashfall. [Alison Pearce Stevens]

Nebraska was once covered with herds of horses. We know this because horse fossils have been found in all parts of the state. Want to find a fossil? Wander along a creek bed or river's edge, and there's a decent chance you'll come across a fossil horse tooth. At one point, Nebraska was home to nine different species of horses. (For comparison, today we have nine species spread all over the world. They include the horses and donkeys that people own, and their wild relatives, including several kinds of zebra.)

At the time of the supervolcanic eruption, there were at least six kinds of horses living near the water hole. The smallest was about the size of a Great Dane dog. Others were quite a bit larger, almost as tall as a grown woman. Some had three toes, while others had just one.

A three-toed horse hoof.

Today's horses all have a single hoof on each foot. You can think of that hoof as a giant toenail, wrapped around the end of a single toe. (That's right—horses run around on tiptoe!) But horses didn't always have just one toe. Some used to have three—a main one with a smaller hoofed toe on either side. And long, *long* ago (fifty-five million years), the very first horses had four toes and walked around like dogs. They even had pads on their feet instead of hooves. Those four-toed horses were tiny—not much bigger than a large housecat.

Why do toes matter? They're good for balance. And especially helpful when turning.

Imagine running through a forest. You have to dodge branches and dart around trees. Your toes spread out, helping to shift your weight as you turn. If you had to make a quick turn on tiptoe, you would probably have a hard time changing direction. If you're a small animal with a predator hot on your tail, you don't have a second to lose to make your getaway.

Believe it or not, the ancient horses of Nebraska did just that. They were small and on the menu for many predators in the area. Unlike the horses found at Poison Ivy Quarry, those ancient horses also lived in forests.

Across the gully from the quarry, Mike found solid evidence of it: a stand of fossilized trees. Sand had buried the ancient trees. Over time, they **petrified**, or turned to stone. Those fossil trees are older than the Poison Ivy animals by one to two million years. Other places in the state not only have similar fossilized forests, they also have fossils of the animals that lived in them, including three-toed horses.

What happened to those forests? The climate changed.

When forests covered Nebraska, it was warm and wet—almost tropical. But then North America got drier. Less rain fell. The forests thinned out and were replaced by grasslands.

Some animals, including horses, began to eat grasses instead of forest plants. But standing in the middle of a big grassy plain makes you an easy target for predators. Instead of hiding, these horses had to *run*! If a horse is bolting in just one direction, it doesn't need those side toes to make quick turns. What's more, horses with a single toe could run faster. That wasn't just because of the single toe. The foot itself changed when it lost the side toes, giving it more spring in each step.

Growing toes (or any other body part) takes a lot of energy. When animals no longer need the body part, it often gets smaller or disappears completely. That doesn't happen in just one animal. It's a slow process that takes place over many generations.

How do we know it happens? Scientists have recorded such changes in animals big and small. One example: Birds on islands lose the ability to fly. Growing long flight feathers and big muscles to power the wings takes lots of energy. Birds on most islands don't have predators. Since they don't need to make a quick escape, they lose the ability to fly.

The horses at Poison Ivy Quarry were in the process of losing those extra toes. If you're imagining that their toes simply fell off, don't worry. It wasn't like that.

A closer look at a three-toed horse hoof.

The paleontologists found that within one species, named the stout one-toed horse, not all horses had one toe. Some did, but others had three on each foot. And some of those three-toed horses had smaller side toes than others. The tiny toes were too short to reach the ground and wouldn't have been useful.

If those horses had lived and had babies, their side toes might have been even smaller. Their grandkids or great-grandkids might not have had any at all. By studying many individuals of the same species, the team could see that the stout one-toed horse hadn't yet become completely one-toed, but it was headed in that direction.

How, when the number of toes varied, did the scientists know those horses all belonged to the same species? Their skulls and teeth.

Scientists use certain features, such as tooth size, shape, and bumps or indentations in the skull, to identify fossils. At Poison Ivy Quarry, the skulls were still attached to the rest of the skeleton, all the way down to the toes. So the team knew exactly how many toes each kind of horse had.

That was a huge discovery. Remember that most fossils are separated (a bone here, a tooth there). Parts of all of these horses had been found in other places across the state. The museum collections were filled with teeth, jaws, skulls, and other bones. Researchers knew they had both one-toed and three-toed horses, but they didn't always know for sure which skulls went with which feet—they had a jumble of bones, with no way to know if they were matching them up correctly.

The new discoveries changed that.

The paleontology team was able to go back to the collections, examine all those individual bones, and reclassify them using the new information. Mystery solved.

DIGGING DEEPER

Removing the skeletons felt wrong to Mike. He felt as though the team were vandalizing the site. If he had been able to, Mike would have left the skeletons in the ground—uncovered and visible, but lying where they had fallen. But he had learned the hard way that leaving them exposed wasn't an option.

Rain and wind easily washed the ash away from the bones. This process of **erosion** exposes fossils along riverbeds and cliffs across the state. It's rather handy most of the time—paleontologists often revisit sites after a good rain to see what new fossils might be poking through.

But at Poison Ivy Quarry, wind and rain were a problem. The bones were so brittle, the ash literally held them together. When it washed away, the bones lost their support and broke into lots of little pieces.

Rain damaged the bones directly, too. The team couldn't leave the skeletons in the ground, where they would get rained on and eventually ruined. When they wrapped up each evening, they covered the fossils with tarps in case of rain. Mike wanted to put up a building to protect them. This would protect them not only from rain, but from freezing in winter. He knew that frost would break them apart. But a protective building wasn't possible. So they removed each skeleton and took it to the museum where it would be safe.

We're used to seeing fossils on display in museums. (What you see in a museum is usually a **replica**—a copy—of the actual fossil.) But the location of a fossil in the ground is incredibly important. The place where it's found gives pale-ontologists all kinds of information. The rock around it can be dated, telling researchers how old the fossil is. Nearby fossils can provide information about climate and the plants and animals that lived in the area. The position of each animal can tell researchers about how ancient rivers moved across the land. The locations of individual bones can also provide clues about what happened to the animals after they died. And the rock surrounding the fossil can even contain chemical traces of the animal's soft tissues—skin or internal organs.

The animals in Poison Ivy Quarry provided much of that information. That was true even after they were taken back to the lab. But their positions in the ground couldn't be saved.

The best the team could do was carefully label every single specimen and record its location on a map of the site before removing the fossil from the quarry. This helped reconstruct some of that on-site information later on.

There was one other benefit to removing the skeletons: Each one that came out revealed new ones hidden underneath. The team worked slowly, removing the skeletons one layer at a time.

And there were still more layers to come.

Underneath the horses and camels, the team found the remains of saber-toothed deer. The deer were smaller than even the smallest horse—only about as tall as a golden retriever dog. They got their name from the long, sharp canines jutting out from the males' slender snouts.

A male saber-toothed deer, named for its long, sharp canines.

Beneath the deer lay the smallest animals—birds and turtles. These animals were at the bottom of the water hole, lying on a thin cushion of ash.

Those layers provided an important clue to what had happened at the time of the eruption. The small animals must have died quickly after the ash cloud arrived. Their small lungs probably filled with ash in a matter of hours. Deer, with their larger lungs, would have survived for days. Horses and camels for a week or two. And the rhinos for more than a month—long enough for Marie's disease to set in.

The birds the team unearthed weren't tiny. Most would have been about the size of a large hawk. But birds have a particularly sensitive **respiratory system**. When they breathe in, some air goes into their lungs. But some also fills air sacs in their bellies. Then, when the birds exhale, the air in those air sacs moves into the lungs. This keeps a constant flow of fresh air moving through their bodies.

Normally, this system works extremely well, pumping oxygen into the bird's body so it can fly long distances. But when the air is filled with ash, it's a different story. It would have taken no time at all for that delicate system to fill with glass shards and come to a screeching halt.

So it's no surprise that Mike and his team found bird skeletons at the very bottom of the quarry, lying just above the sandy floor of the water hole. Ash falling from the sky probably landed on the water and settled to the bottom, covering—and protecting—their delicate bones. What *was* surprising: how many bird skeletons had fossilized at all.

Bird bones don't typically fossilize well. That's probably because they're hollow. Hollow bones are both light and strong, which makes it easier for birds to fly. Although hollow bones are perfect for flight, they don't make good fossils. Their thin walls are easily crushed. So finding an entire bird skeleton is unusual.

Even so, dozens upon dozens of birds have been unearthed in Poison Ivy Quarry. In one part of the ash bed, the paleontologists found a flock of forty birds. (Mike, who specialized in mammals, didn't know what kind of birds they were. He sent them to a specialist after the dig was done.) Many of the skeletons had been crushed, trampled by larger animals as they sought relief in the water hole. But a few were intact, with all bones in place. Feathers had left impressions in the ash. Even the rings of **cartilage** in their necks were perfectly preserved.

Cartilage is softer than bone. It's the rubbery stuff that gives shape to your ears and the tip of your nose. If you touch the front of your neck, you'll feel a thick tube running from top to bottom. That's your **trachea**. It's the breathing tube that connects your lungs to your nose and mouth. Rings of cartilage hold it open (you can feel these, too!), so you have a clear path for air to move in and out. These are the same rings that the paleontologists found for many of the birds.

EUREKA!

The birds were an especially exciting discovery for the team. Paleontologists in Nebraska had been finding fossils of rhinos, horses, and camels for more than one hundred years. In fact, the sheer number of rhino skulls found in the state might be the reason why Donald Peterson's discovery sat neglected at the museum all those years.

The birds, on the other hand, were completely unknown before the dig at Poison Ivy Quarry. The team didn't know that right away. Not until later, after Alan Feduccia had taken a closer look. A bird paleontologist at the University of North Carolina, Alan was an expert in ancient birds. That meant he was also an expert in modern birds. Understanding the skeletons and body structures of modern birds helped him figure out the ancient ones.

Alan took lots of measurements of the bones. He looked at their shapes, including any indentations, holes, or bumps. He studied fossil skeletons that had already been identified and examined skeletons from modern birds that might be similar. Alan compared them all, looking for things that were similar or different from other, known, species.

In the end, he was delighted to find not one but *three* new species.

One was a type of vulture. Another turned out to be a long-legged hawk, similar to the secretary bird that currently lives in Africa. Alan didn't have an entire skeleton to study for this hawk, just a single foot. But it was enough for him to figure out that the fossil bird, even though it resembled the secretary bird, was actually something else.

Sometimes animals and plants that aren't related look similar. This is called **convergent evolution**. It happens when they live in similar types of habitats—even if those habitats are very far apart. Over time, as species adapt to their environments, similar features might be useful in a particular environment. So those features occur in both organisms, even though the species are not related, nor do they live near each other.

For example, most people in the Americas recognize hummingbirds by their long, curved beaks and rapid wing beats (those fluttering wings are what create the "hum").

Hummingbirds drink nectar, and they prefer to do so from long, trumpet-shaped flowers.

There aren't many animals that can reach the nectar in these flowers, so hummingbirds with longer bills have the advantage. Long ago, they started specializing on these flowers. Birds with longer bills got more food and were able to raise more young. Those young inherited the longer beaks and were also able to raise more young. Beaks got longer from one generation to the next. Over time, we ended up with the long-billed hummingbirds we see today. (That change in the population is what we call **evolution**.)

Trumpet-shaped flowers exist in other parts of the world— places where there are no hummingbirds. But that doesn't mean there aren't birds that sip nectar from deep inside. In Southeast Asia, such flowers are visited by long-beaked birds that look a lot like hummingbirds. They're about the same size, just as brightly colored, and have long, curved bills. But they're not hummingbirds. They're sunbirds. And they're more closely related to crows than they are to hummingbirds.

It was a similar case of convergent evolution that Alan uncovered when he investigated the first bird fossil.

Secretary birds are unusual; they have extremely long legs. They stalk the savanna, searching for prey: snakes, lizards, turtles, large insects, and small birds and mammals. When a bird finds one, it attacks—with its feet!

Secretary birds are terrific stompers. They can hit the ground (or their intended dinner) with a force equal to five times their own body weight. A large secretary bird weighs almost ten pounds—imagine having a fifty-pound weight dropped on your head.

A long-legged hawk, similar to the secretary bird.

The hawk from Poison Ivy Quarry had similarly long feet. It probably hunted the same way. But its toes were like a hawk's toes. Since only the main foot bone (the one that connected the ankle to the rest of the foot) resembled the secretary bird, Alan deduced that this was a case of convergent evolution. This was a different, unrelated type of bird that had evolved a similar approach to catching dinner.

In another part of the water hole, the team had discovered

a flock of forty crane-like birds. Mike initially suspected they were an ancestor of sandhill cranes.

Sandhill cranes stop in Nebraska on their way north each spring. Hundreds of thousands of them gather on the Platte River in March. A river overflowing with large birds? It's one of the biggest wildlife spectacles in the United States, and people flock to the area to watch them each year.

Like most cranes, sandhill cranes migrate long distances, building nests thousands of miles away from where they spend the winter. Crowned cranes are the exception. These birds spend their lives near water holes in the middle of the African savanna. They move around some, but they don't migrate. Instead they stay near the rhinos and zebras and— Hmm . . . sounds a bit like the animals at Poison Ivy Quarry!

So what *had* the team found? Alan examined the bones of six different fossil skeletons. (He couldn't use a single skeleton, because the rhinos had crushed at least part of each one.) Right away, he spotted features found only in crowned cranes.

The trachea was straight instead of twisted. That alone was an extraordinary discovery that was possible only because the ash had preserved those rings of cartilage. The breastbone was solid. Migrating cranes have holes in their breastbones that the trachea winds through. The beak was short, instead of long and pointed. Even the wing and leg bones were similar to those of an African crowned crane.

Alan deduced that the Poison Ivy birds were crowned

cranes. But they were a new species of crowned crane. The skeletons had several differences from the African birds, so he knew they weren't exactly the same, but they were a close cousin.

A crowned crane, notable because, unlike other cranes, it doesn't migrate.

He was even more confident about this discovery when he looked at the rest of Poison Ivy Quarry. To have crowned cranes hanging out at a water hole in the middle of a savanna with lots of grassland animals—that fits right in with what we know about their modern relatives.

SEEING A BIGGER PICTURE

After months of hard work, the team reached the bottom of the ash bed. The soft, gray ash gave way to rough, yellowish sandstone. Their work appeared to be finished.

But it wasn't.

The team dusted away ash from the uneven bed, revealing footprints. Big, blobby rhino tracks crisscrossed the once-muddy area. Tracks can form only when the ground is soggy, as it is after a big rain or at the edges of a pond or lake. Although Mike had begun to suspect that the animals had died in a water hole, this was the first time he'd seen evidence of it.

The sandstone below held all kinds of fossils, most of which were different from those in the ash. These were fully mineralized, like most fossils. And, like most fossils, they were incomplete. Individual bones and teeth emerged, the remnants of a wide variety of critters: turtles, salamanders, snakes, lizards, and birds. All kinds of mammals, too, ranging from tiny rodents to massive four-tusked elephants. For the first time, the team found fossils of predators—six kinds of dogs had visited the water hole, as had beardogs.

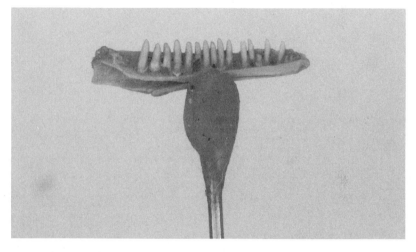

A microfossil of a fence lizard's jawbone, found near the crane that had swallowed it. [Shane Tucker]

All of these animals had lived near the water hole before the eruption blanketed the area with ash. The same species were also around at the time of the eruption, but they hadn't died in the water hole the way the rhinos and horses had. The older bones had settled in the sandy bottom, where water flowed freely. There they soaked up minerals and eventually turned stone-like.

After removing the easy-to-spot fossils, the team carefully sifted shovelful after shovelful of sand through mesh screens. This allowed them to find incredibly tiny fossils (called **microfossils**) they had overlooked—an itty-bitty tooth from a mouse, vertebrae from a snake, even tiny grass seeds. They had done the same thing with the ash but hadn't found any microfossils in that layer.

A microfossil of a horned rodent's tooth that lay hidden in the sand below the ash. [Shane Tucker]

In the sandstone, however, they found a treasure trove.

Once they removed the last of the fossils from the site, the team headed home. Their summer field season was over.

Fall was coming, and with it came a new phase of research: time in the collections. The team had more than three hundred jacketed fossils that needed to be opened, cleaned up, and studied. And they had an abundance of microfossils to identify, as well.

When they got the specimens back to the lab, the paleontologists set to work.

Normally, when scientists prepare a fossil, they open the field jacket and free one side from the surrounding rock, then flip the whole thing over and clean the other side. A fully prepared fossil is usually free of both its field jacket and the rock in which it was found. This was the process the team followed for fossils found in the sandstone below the ash.

But the skeletons from the ash layer weren't strong enough to get the full treatment. They needed the support of the ash to keep them from crumbling. So the museum staff prepared only half of each one. The partial preparation exposed rounded ribs, slender toes, and other bones while leaving enough ash to support the delicate fossils.

The researchers couldn't inspect the other side of the fossils, but the specimens didn't fall apart, either!

At last, Mike was able to carefully examine each specimen. He studied the knobs and indentations on the bones, scraped ash from between teeth, and discovered bits of the animals' last meals inside their rib cages.

One of the cranes had eaten a small lizard shortly before the ash had fallen. That tiny skeleton was the only lizard found in the ash layer, although bones and teeth from other lizards came out of the sandstone below.

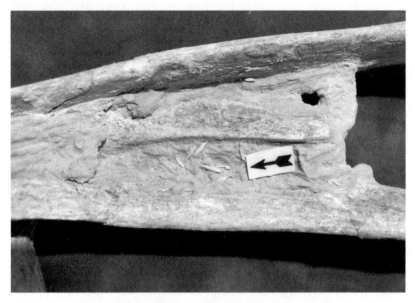

The arrow points to fossilized grass seeds
found in this rhino's hyoid bone. [Rick Otto]

A female rhino had fossilized grass seeds stuck to her tongue bone. (A bone called the **hyoid** [hi-oyd] attaches the tongue to the jaw at the front of the neck.) Another female had fossilized seeds where her stomach had once been. And some rhinos could have used dental floss—they still had seeds stuck in between their teeth!

Sandwiched between the ash and underlying sand, the team had found similar seeds. They had discovered others in the sandstone. Mike knew mammals, but not plants, and he knew he needed help to identify them.

Two **paleobotanists**—experts in ancient plants—stepped up. Peg Bolick specialized in fossil pollen at the University of Nebraska State Museum. And Joe Thomasson was an expert in fossil plants at Fort Hays State University in Kansas. Together, they worked to identify the different kinds of plants. Fossilized stems don't offer a lot of information, but seeds and pollen have distinctive shapes and features that make them easy to identify—if you know what you're looking for.

Peg was something of a trailblazer in her field, pioneering new techniques. And she was extremely good at finding pollen in places others hadn't thought to look.

She had already helped Mike find fossil pollen by checking inside a young mammoth's sinuses. The mammoth wasn't from Poison Ivy Quarry. It had lived during the Ice Age, about half a million years ago. Mike was part of the team that found the mammoth and brought it to the museum.

Peg suffered from terrible allergies. She knew—from every sneeze and sniffle—that many types of pollen are tiny enough to travel on a puff of wind. When someone breathes them in, they can cause an allergic reaction. *Aaa-choo!* She also knew that the sinuses are a good place for that pollen to get stuck. So she used a swab to swipe the inside of the mammoth's sinus cavities. She added a few drops of water to the swab, rubbed it on a slide, and took a peek under the microscope. Lo and behold: pollen!

Peg and Mike tried the swab with other Ice Age fossils:

mastodons, giant bison, and other species that lived in the cold. All of them had pollen trapped inside their sinuses. Peg studied the pollen. She found that during the Ice Age, Nebraska had been covered with trees. In fact, Nebraska at that time looked a lot like Minnesota does today.

Because they'd had such good success swabbing Ice Age nostrils, Peg wanted to try it with the rhinos. She swabbed the sinuses of one and checked under the microscope. Lots of ash, but no pollen. She swabbed another. Still none. Peg checked them all, but none of the skulls from Poison Ivy Quarry had pollen packed—or even sprinkled—inside.

The cold conditions during the Ice Age had helped preserve that pollen, keeping it whole while it fossilized. The Poison Ivy Quarry animals lived in a warmer climate. Any pollen that might have been in their sinuses decayed before it could harden with minerals. It was a major disappointment for everyone involved.

Fortunately, the team still had the seeds and other fossilized plant parts. Joe was particularly good at finding seeds. He scooped ash into a bucket of water. The ash sank while the fossil seeds—which were hollow—floated to the top. Joe skimmed them off, dried them, and studied them using a **scanning electron microscope**.

The most common microscope is a light microscope. This uses a bright light to make tiny objects easy to see through a series of magnifying lenses. Light microscopes work well with transparent objects, like cells. Moving the object closer to or farther from the lens lets the viewer see internal structures.

A scanning electron microscope (SEM for short) doesn't use light. Instead, it sends a beam of high-energy **electrons** at tiny objects. These interact with the outside of the specimen, creating highly detailed images of it. SEM is handy when objects are really small and when the objects have a lot of detailed outer structures. It's not useful for peering inside. But it's perfect for studying things like pollen and grass seeds.

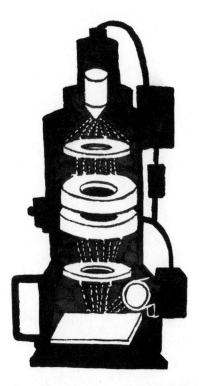

A scanning electron microscope (SEM), which
sends a beam of high-energy electrons at tiny
objects to create detailed images of them.

Joe took images of the seeds using the SEM. He had other microfossils, too—fruit-like structures that once housed seeds. The SEM images showed that the fossils had been preserved with incredible detail. Tiny bumps, holes, cracks, lines, and more appeared in the images. Many of these made it possible for Joe to identify which species of plants had produced the seeds and fruits.

Almost all of his samples were full of long, thin grass seeds. One in particular seemed to be a favorite food for the rhinos—this grass was found on or in every rhino that had a fossilized last meal. And no wonder—it was the most common grass throughout all of the samples Joe tested. (The grass doesn't have a common name, just a scientific one: *Berriochloa communis* [berry-oh-KLOW-uh COM-you-nis]. Grasses are often named for their appearance, but we don't know what this one looked like!) Joe found the grass on the rhino fossils, in the layer between the ash and sandstone, and down in the sandstone, as well. In that bottom layer, he also found horsetail, other types of grasses, grass-like sedges, some flowering plants, and walnuts and hackberries.

Joe's studies provided a picture of what the environment had been like at the time of the eruption: a savanna with lots of grasses and other grass-like plants dotted here and there with trees and shrubs.

The researchers now had evidence that the area was a thriving ecosystem, with plants and animals big and small living together—and sometimes eating each other.

MAKING A PARK

After the two summers of digging, excavation came to a halt. Money had run out, and Mike had decided he wouldn't excavate any more unless he could leave the skeletons in place. He had plenty to keep him busy in the collections, though, and he spent the next several summers uncovering fossils in other parts of the state.

But things were still happening. *National Geographic* magazine ran a story about Poison Ivy Quarry that got the attention of some people in Omaha (a good three hours away). They wanted the site to be a state park, which would preserve and protect it for years to come. So they bought the ranch, including the quarry, and donated it to the state of Nebraska.

Excavator Mary Ann Jones works at the
Poison Ivy Quarry, soon to be renamed the
Ashfall Fossil Beds. [Annie Griffiths]

Parks are public places, and a spot named after poison
ivy wasn't likely to draw many visitors, so the state renamed
it. Poison Ivy Quarry became Ashfall Fossil Beds State Histor-
ical Park. That's a mouthful, so everyone just called it Ashfall.

Mike was thrilled.

Having Ashfall as a state park would allow researchers to

work there as long as there were fossils to find. A landowner couldn't decide to keep them off the land or keep the fossils for themselves. And the site could be protected from damage and theft.

At the same time, they needed to let people visit the site and even watch while the paleontologists worked. In the past, people who lived nearby would hang out on a nearby hilltop and watch, sometimes while enjoying a picnic lunch. That had worked for a short while, but if the digging were going to continue, things needed to be more controlled.

Mike had a solution.

He'd been dreaming for nearly a decade of putting a protective barn over the site. That would let the team excavate new skeletons without having to remove them. A barn would protect the fossils from the weather, as well as from people and animals. A walkway around the inside of the barn would let visitors get a good, close-up view of the skeletons—without getting *too* close.

But where to put the barn?

The original team had cleared only a small part of the hillside. They had removed everything in that area; there was nothing left to find, although they saw hints of more skeletons along the edges. Any new digging would have to take place off to one side or another, in a different part of the water hole.

Mike and some of his students needed to find the best location to build, so they picked up their shovels and got to work.

The team dug a grid of trenches across an area the size

of five basketball courts. In some trenches they found fossils. In others, there were none.

Mike asked the state for a building the size of three basketball courts to cover the promising spots in the ash bed. But there wasn't enough money for a building that big. In the end, they put up a much smaller barn, just thirty by sixty feet in size. Dubbed the Rhino Barn, it had a wooden walkway for visitors that ran around the inside of the walls, hovering over the top of the ash.

The Rhino Barn, built over a section
of the Ashfall Fossil Beds.

By the time the barn was finished, eleven years had passed since the big excavation.

Mike was itching to get back to work.

Inside the barn, the work started once again. Mike and Rick Otto recruited **interns**—college students who were training to be paleontologists. Rick had helped with the big dig years before and was now the park superintendent.

A group of five or six interns came out that summer, and a new group has arrived each summer since. Each intern worked in their own square, about five feet across. They scraped away the ash under the watchful eye of Mike and Rick—and the tens of thousands of visitors who came to observe.

Their process was much like the one Mike's team followed during the big excavation. The interns removed ash quickly at first, filling buckets that they then dumped into a gully. All of the previous fossils had been found in the bottom three feet of ash, so they knew it was safe to work fast. But as they got closer to the lower layer, they slowed, switching to brushes and dental tools when they found a fossil.

The big difference: There were no plaster jackets; no fossils removed from the site. No one had to cart one-ton fossils off to the museum collections.

Instead, the interns cleaned the skeletons in place, carefully clearing away the ash, leaving each skeleton supported by a pedestal of gray powder. They exposed as much as they could, digging deeper next to each skeleton to see if anything else was buried beneath. More often than not, they hit the jackpot.

Just like the first excavation, rhinos lay on top. Those were the first skeletons found as the interns began to dig. But some of those rhinos lay on top of horses and camels. One intern cleaned off a rhino skeleton only to find a horse's head sticking out from underneath one side and its hind feet poking out the other. Below it lay a saber-toothed deer.

Rhino skeletons fill this area of the ashbed. These are some of the first skeletons uncovered by Voorhies's team. [Alison Pearce Stevens]

Dozens and dozens of skeletons lay crowded together, couched in their blanket of ash. As in the first dig, the animals were layered by size, with the biggest on top.

Each new discovery happened right in front of park visitors. They asked questions and the interns explained what it all meant.

Hundreds of animals had died after the eruption. They had all gathered in this place that had become their deathbed.

SEARCHING FOR ANCIENT WATER

When interns found skeletons, they couldn't dig too deep or they risked damaging the fossils. To this day, no one knows what—if anything—lies beneath the exposed skeletal remains.

But some interns found fewer fossils in the ash. They dug all the way to the sand underneath. There they found more evidence that the ash had settled into water.

Along the edges, where the ash thinned out, they found fossilized ripples. Ripples happen only when there's water, more confirmation that the area had once been wet. But water can be still, as in a pond, or it can flow, like a stream or river. What kind of water had the animals come to visit?

The ripples were symmetrical. The peak of each one sat directly between the valleys on either side. Such symmetrical ripples happen only when wind blows across shallow water. When water flows over the ground—in a stream or when the ocean's tide goes out—the peaks of the ripples are off to one side. The water pushes them in that direction as it goes by. Symmetrical ripples confirmed that the site had once been a water hole.

Mike figured it must have been filled by rain, rather than fed by a stream or river. Modern rain-fed water holes dry up during the dry season; this ancient one probably did, too. That was guesswork, though, at least for a time. It was another twenty years before Mike knew for sure.

Those answers came after Mike invited Eugene "Gene" Stoermer to come visit. Gene was an expert on **diatoms**. These are tiny, plant-like **algae** that make shells out of glass. Diatoms are found in all water, everywhere on Earth. (They're even found in muddy ground and on the feathers of some diving birds!) Mike knew the water hole had once held water. So it made sense that it had also once had diatoms.

Diatoms are among the most important, and least known, organisms on our planet.

Like plants, they turn sunlight and carbon dioxide into food and oxygen. There are so many of these itty-bitty algae, they produce about one quarter of the oxygen we breathe. (That's one out of every four breaths you take.) They're the base of the food chain in oceans. People even use their shells to filter swimming pool water, french fry oil, and other things.

The freshwater diatom *Aulacoseira*, found in the ash, is evidence that the water hole was filled with water at the time of the ashfall. [Mark Edlund]

Diatoms are wonderfully easy to study, too.

Different species make glass houses with different shapes, openings, and other features. That makes them easy to identify—if you know what you're looking for.

Gene collected samples from the ash and took them back to his lab at the University of Michigan. Sure enough, he found the beautiful glass houses of many kinds of diatoms.

Gene, who taught a class on diatoms in Iowa each year, decided that Ashfall would be the perfect place for a field trip.

The next year, he and his assistant, Mark Edlund, took their students to Ashfall. It's a field trip Mark—who now teaches the class—has taken every year since.

Each year, the students collect samples from the ash. They take some from the ash itself, near newly discovered skeletons or along the edge of the ash bed. They take others from the sand below the ash. They don't take much, just a few spoonfuls from each location. Many students find it strange that they are taking such small samples next to such big fossils. But since the diatoms are smaller than the width of a human hair, that's really all they need.

They take their samples back to Iowa Lakeside Laboratory. The students spread the ash on glass slides and study them under light microscopes, scanning back and forth, back and forth, searching for diatom shells. It can be slow and frustrating, since diatom shells and the volcanic ash are both made of glass. (It doesn't help that there's a *lot* more ash than diatoms!)

But even after a long search, they almost always find some. They usually find quite a few diatoms in the samples taken from the sandy bottom. They find fewer in the ash samples. Samples taken close to the bottom of the water hole—from the ash right above the sand—usually have more.

The diatom *Alveolophora* was also found in the ash layer. This image shows a single diatom, but *Alveolophora* were often strung together in long chains when they were alive. [Mark Edlund]

That actually makes a lot of sense. A diatom's glass house might be tiny, but it still weighs the diatom down. It relies on wind blowing across the water to churn things up, lifting the diatom closer to the surface. There, it can get good sunlight for **photosynthesis**. But when the wind stops, the diatom sinks again. It's kind of like a glass bottle sinking in a lake (only a whole lot smaller!). As ash filled the water hole, diatoms— like the seeds—would have been trapped at the bottom.

The diatoms the students find aren't quite like any that exist now. Just like other living things, diatoms evolve over time. Some go extinct. But their relatives might survive. So

Mark and his students use what they know about modern diatoms to understand the ones they find at Ashfall. (Just like Mike did with the rhinos and Alan did with the birds.)

Diatoms from the ash looked a lot like modern ones that are found only in freshwater. This was an important discovery. It meant that the water hole had water in it when the volcano erupted. It was just as Mike suspected: The ash storm must have happened during a rainy season. One question answered.

But did the water hole *always* have water in it?

To find out, the students looked at the diatoms from the sand below the ash. The sand holds the record of life in the area *before* the eruption. Mike's team had found all kinds of plants and animals in the sand that they didn't find in the ash.

Diatoms were no different.

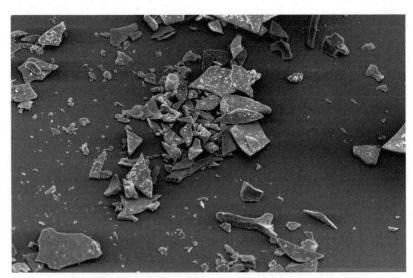

Mark Edlund and his students had to find cylindrical diatoms scattered throughout the glassy ash. There is one diatom in this image—can you find it? [Mark Edlund]

Mark's students found more kinds of diatoms in the sand than they did in the ash. Some of the same freshwater species found in the ash were also in the sand. But the sand held other kinds of diatoms, too. These other ones only like salty water. They can't survive in freshwater. Finding them there was a huge clue—it meant the water hole sometimes dried up.

When water evaporates, only the water molecules break off into the air. Anything else in the water—like salt—gets left behind. As more and more water evaporates, what's left gets saltier and saltier. At some point, it's salty enough for those salty diatoms to thrive. But where did they come from?

Diatoms make resting **spores** when the environment isn't right for them. These spores have thick outer walls that are both protective and heavy. The freshwater species created resting spores when it got too salty. Those spores would rest on the bottom of the water hole until it filled up again.

In the same way, the salt-loving species rested in their spores until the water level got low. When it got good and salty, they would come out of their spores and go back to turning sunlight into food and oxygen.

Mark's students' findings added to the story Mike had been piecing together.

It was now clear that the water hole had filled with water during the rainy season and dried up when the rains stopped. It had been an important source of water for a wide variety of animals living in the area—so important that animals sought it out when the ash made them sick.

THE LUCKY ONES

Was it simply ash floating through the air that did the animals in? That may have been the case for the smaller critters, but Mike didn't think that was what killed the big ones.

He knew from fossils found above and below the ash layer that many different kinds of animals lived in the area at the time of the eruption. Only a handful of those species had been found in the ash.

Clearly, size was a factor. But Mike noticed another curious pattern: All of the larger skeletons came from animals that ate grass.

There was no question that the rhinos ate grass—they had fossilized food wedged between their teeth! Even though the team didn't find grass seeds on or in the horse skeletons, they still knew the five horse species in the ash ate grass, just like the rhinos did. How did they know?

By their teeth.

We're lucky to have hands. They let us do things like harvest our food, rather than eating it straight from the plant. So we can clean our food before shoveling it into our mouths. Some other animals do this—monkeys, apes, and raccoons, for example—but most other animals aren't so lucky. They chomp on leaves and grass, using their lips and tongues to grab and their teeth to tear. Any dust, dirt, or sand that's on the leaves goes in their mouths, too. When these animals chew, those bits of grit gouge pits and scratches into their teeth.

Ever gotten sand in your sandwich? You know what it feels like.

Teeth wear down faster in animals that eat grass (called **grazers**) than in animals that nibble leaves off shrubs and trees (called **browsers**). One reason: Grazers pick up lots of grit when they eat. After all, their food is right down there in the dirt! But there's another reason. Grass itself is hard on teeth.

Teeth are tough. They're made from enamel, which is the hardest substance in the body. But animals that eat grass have a tough time of it. Grasses contain lots of glass-like silica in them. Silica is the same stuff that makes up sand (and the glass houses of diatoms). Scientists think grasses have silica to help protect themselves from being eaten. It works—against some animals, such as insects. Not so much with big herbivores like rhinos and horses. They mow down meadows, grinding grass day in and day out.

That's bad news for their teeth, which wear away gradually over time.

Teeth that belong to grazers, animals that eat grass.

Once an animal's teeth get too short, it can't eat anymore. That means animals with taller teeth can live longer. Scientists find a clear difference in tooth type for modern grazers and browsers. For example, modern horses eat grass. They also have extremely tall teeth. Modern deer are browsers, and their teeth are much shorter. Knowing how tooth shape relates to diet in living animals provides a big clue to paleontologists studying ancient critters.

Every single rhino they had uncovered belonged to the same species: the barrel-bodied rhino. This species of rhino can be identified in part by tall teeth. But barrel-bodied rhinos weren't the only rhinos around at the time. Hornless rhinos also lived on the Great Plains. Individual teeth and bones turned up in the sandstone above and below the ash. But not a single hornless rhino ended up in the water hole.

The same was true of horses. Six species of horses lived in the area at the time of the eruption. Only five were found in the ash. Fossils of the sixth species, like the hornless rhino, are limited to individual teeth and bones found in the sandstone.

How is it that two species could escape the fate met by the rest of the animals? Their teeth may provide an answer. Barrel-bodied rhinos and those five species of horses share something in common: They all have the tall teeth found only in grazers. Hornless rhinos and the sixth species of horse were browsers.

What does all that have to do with animals dying from volcanic ash?

The ash settled over the ground, covering everything in about a foot of soft gray fluff. It buried the grasses. Grazers had to dig through it in order to eat, much like caribou dig through snow to find food in winter. Now, instead of just grinding on grit when they dined, they were taking in ash by the mouthful. Their noses were right down there in the deadly fluff, too.

Researchers think that's what happened: Grazers probably breathed in much more ash than the browsers did. Those lucky leaf-eaters could shake the ash off branches before they munched their lunch. Although they surely breathed in *some* ash, it probably wasn't nearly as much as the grazers did.

Not enough to kill them.

FINDING THE VOLCANO

As interns continued to uncover new skeletons, other researchers visited Ashfall, too.

Scientists with the United States Geological Survey wanted to know how big the water hole was. To find out, they pounded **electrodes** into the ground in areas that were still covered with rock, soil, and plants. These were placed every two to three feet. Then they connected them all with a cable and shot electricity through the electrodes and into the ground.

Like radio waves, electricity moves through different kinds of rock at different speeds. The scientists didn't find evidence of fossils, but then, they weren't looking for them, either. They *were* able to see how deep the ash was. By finding the places where it thinned out, they figured out the water hole went far into the hillside—well beyond the walls of the Rhino Barn.

In 2006, USGS scientists ran electricity through in-ground electrodes for their electric resistance imaging survey. [Rick Otto]

Specialists in ash came to visit, too. Michael Perkins, a geologist at the University of Utah, knew volcanic ash. He knew the gray fluff well enough that he could tell where it came from. (Not by looking. He tested the ash to see what chemicals were inside.)

Remember that Mike Voorhies had guessed at both the age of the Ashfall animals and the location of the super-volcano that buried them. He thought the ash had probably come from volcanoes in New Mexico, which were active about ten million years ago. That time frame fit with the time when rhinos, horses, and camels roamed across the Great Plains.

It wasn't a stab in the dark—Mike had used the information that was available at the time to make those estimates. But he knew he needed something more definitive. Michael Perkins was able to provide the necessary data.

Perkins had been studying layers of volcanic ash found in the states around Utah. He collected ash from all over the place: Utah, Idaho, Montana, Wyoming, Washington, Oregon, Nevada, and California. He measured the ash layers, recording how thick they were, and he analyzed the ash, breaking it down to see which chemicals it contained.

He discovered some interesting things.

When a volcano erupts, the ash falls out in much thicker layers closer to the eruption. Those layers thin out the farther away from the volcano you get. By looking at the thickness of the ash layers, Perkins realized that most of the ash had come from a swath of volcanoes that had existed across southern Idaho long, long ago.

That was strong evidence by itself. But Perkins wanted to be absolutely certain. He ran chemical tests on the ash and found that ash from each eruption had its own chemical signature. The ash from one eruption was chemically different from the ash shot out of the volcano the next time it blew—even when the eruption came out of the same spot. This let Perkins say for certain that ash found in, say, northern Utah, had come from an eruption in the southwestern part of Idaho.

Scientists had already identified seven different volcanic **calderas**, or massive areas that had once been the site of eruptions. These spanned southern Idaho, from Oregon to Wyoming. But they didn't yet know when those volcanoes had been active.

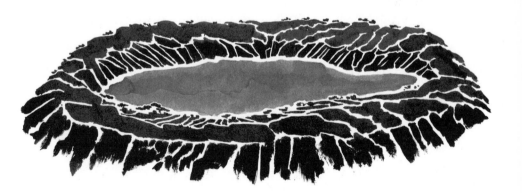

A caldera, a massive area that was
once the site of an eruption.

Perkins's chemical analyses revealed argon in the ash. Argon is radioactive. It's one of many different elements used in radioactive dating. It was just what he needed to figure out how long ago the volcanoes had erupted.

He found that the oldest ash came from volcanic eruptions along the Idaho-Oregon border. The youngest ash came from the easternmost edge of Idaho, right at the Wyoming border. The line of volcanoes had been active over time, with the oldest to the west, youngest to the east, and a gradual transition in between.

That information told Perkins that each volcano had formed over a **hotspot**—an area of superheated magma beneath Earth's crust. The argon dating showed that those seven volcanoes weren't active at the same time—as one went extinct, the next one came to life. Perkins figured the volcanoes popped up in new places because of **plate tectonics**.

Geologists have suspected for more than one hundred years that Earth's surface isn't as immovable as it seems. How else to explain the eastern part of Africa, where magma seeps into a massive rift, forcing the continent to grow wider? Or the way the Atlantic Ocean spreads by one to two inches each year? Or off the coast of California, where one piece of crust is crushed beneath another, sending ripples of earthquakes throughout the region?

Earth's crust is made up of more than fourteen different plates. Some are enormous—the size of North America or the Pacific Ocean, for example—whereas others are much smaller. Each one travels slowly, pushed from underneath by a current of magma. (Even though it is super hot and extremely thick, magma has currents, just like the ocean does.)

When thinner plates collide, such as those under the ocean, one pushes the other one deep, deep into the earth's **mantle**. This can create trenches, like the Mariana Trench near Guam and the Philippines. (The deepest part of that trench lies almost seven miles below the ocean's surface!) When thicker land plates collide, one may get pushed under, but it in turn pushes the other one higher and higher, creating a mountain range.

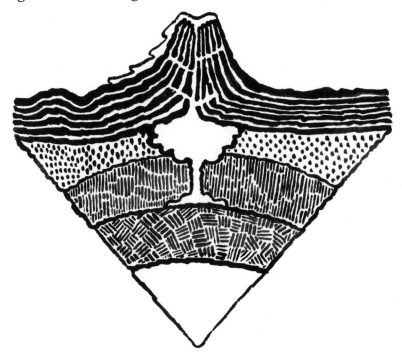

Earth's crust (outer layer) and mantle (inner layers).

North America has been moving oh so slowly west-southwest, moving one to two inches per year. (If that number sounds familiar, that's because the Atlantic Ocean grows wider by the same amount. Those two things go together. The rift in the Atlantic is pushing North America away from Europe.)

The path of the North American Plate lines up perfectly with the line of volcanoes across southern Idaho. As the section of crust moved, it traveled over that hotspot. The superheated magma moved up through the underside of the crust, building up pressure until *KABOOM*! A supervolanic eruption.

The first spot erupted several times before the tectonic plate moved. A new area then sat above the hotspot, creating a whole new set of volcanoes and eruptions. And so on.

You can see the same thing today if you look at the Hawaiian Islands. Hawaii sits in the middle of the Pacific Plate, which moves northwest at a rapid three to four inches per year. (Remember, we're talking about rock here—that's practically sprinting!) Each island was formed as the plate passed over a hotspot, much like the one in Idaho. Over time, the volcano that built up one island would go extinct. Soon, another island would spring up from the depths of the ocean, fed by the hotspot in its new location.

You can't see them all, but there are actually eighty volcanic mountains in the chain of the Hawaiian Islands. They stretch 1,600 miles—all the way to Alaska! Most are completely hidden underwater. Only the tallest and youngest ones have tops that jut out into the air, creating the islands we can see. Older ones have eroded from rain, wind, and pounding waves, gradually disappearing into the ocean.

Mike knew about Perkins's research and wondered if he had any information about the origin of the Ashfall ash.

Perkins collected ash from several places in Nebraska, including Ashfall. He also got ash from New Mexico. He needed to see if the Ashfall ash might have come from the New Mexico volcanoes, like Mike had suspected.

The chemicals in the Ashfall ash didn't match the New Mexico volcanoes. But they perfectly matched one of the ones in Idaho. Named the Bruneau-Jarbidge (after two rivers that meet in the area), this volcano was active from thirteen million to ten million years ago. That fit with the ten-million-year time frame Mike had suspected.

When Perkins dated the Ashfall ash using argon, he came back with a date right in the middle—11.93 million years ago (that's 11,930,000 years). The Ashfall animals had died even earlier than Mike had originally suspected.

That didn't mean his estimate was wrong.

Remember that the fission track data from John Boellstorff put Ashfall ash at 10.5 million years old—*plus or minus* 1.5 million. It was a range of dates, and the new argon study fit right in at just under twelve million years old. Mike now had two sets of data giving him the same information.

PEERING
UNDERGROUND

One summer, Kate McKinley and Erin Wallin drove out to Ashfall. Students at the Colorado School of Mines, they planned to search for fossils using **ground-penetrating radar** (**GPR** for short). If the GPR worked, they would be able to spot fossils before anyone started to dig.

Radar works by sending out high-frequency radio waves. This is the same kind of wave used by radio stations (but GPR uses higher-frequency waves that travel faster). A radio station's number even tells you the frequency of its signal. One radio station might be 91.1 and another 107.3. Those numbers are how many times (multiplied by a thousand) the waves go from high to low each second.

We can't hear GPR's high-frequency waves in our ears.

Instead, the waves bounce off objects. It's a lot like a bat using **sonar**. When the signal bounces off, it creates an echo. Bats can pick up those echoes with their big ears. For radar, the signal is picked up by an antenna.

How can radio waves show us what's underground? After all, when a bat uses its sonar, the sound waves move through air and bounce off physical objects. But ground-penetrating radar sends radio waves straight into the ground—which is solid!

Believe it or not, it doesn't just bounce back as a flat image.

Those radio waves travel at different speeds through different kinds of materials. That means the signals come back at different times. This creates an image of where things are located underground.

GPR is used for lots of things, such as locating pipes and cables buried underground or searching for evidence when a crime has been committed. It's also used by geologists to see where different types of rock lie underground. It's especially useful for finding fossils buried in sandstone. When a bone or tooth has been fully fossilized, it's packed with minerals. It's much more **dense** than the hard-packed sand around it and creates a clear signal that something is there.

Kate and Erin (and a local Girl Scout troop that came to help) walked back and forth, again and again, over the area. Everyone expected the geologists to say "Got something!" at any moment.

Geophysicist George Tsoflias uses ground-penetrating
radar to search for new fossils. [Rick Otto]

But that moment never came.

Because the Ashfall fossils hadn't mineralized, they were the same **density** as the ash around them. The radio waves traveled through both ash and bone at the same speed, giving the researchers a blank map, rather than one dotted with hidden skeletons.

A BIGGER BARN

More than a decade after the Rhino Barn opened, the entire area inside had been excavated; there wasn't anything left to uncover. Mike figured that left them with two options: close the park or build a bigger barn. He desperately wanted to keep the park open.

He and Rick applied for money to expand the barn. But time and again, they were turned down. No one was willing to give them the money they needed.

Discouraged, Mike prepared himself for the worst.

There just wasn't any point in keeping the park open if there wasn't any digging going on. People liked to see fossils, but they liked seeing new things and interacting with researchers even more.

Ashfall was almost three hours from the nearest big city; people who visited went out of their way to do so. Without active digging, the steady stream of visitors would grind to a halt.

One day, Mike received a surprise visit at his office in Lincoln. Ted Hubbard knew about Ashfall and knew Mike needed money to expand the barn. Ted's family often donated to places that helped schoolkids learn about nature and science, and he wanted to know how he could help. Mike told him what they needed.

Ted, his wife, and his sister traveled to Ashfall to get a feel for the place. They happened to arrive during a visit by students from a nearby school. Rick's assistant, Sandy Mosel, was talking to second graders about the skeletons in the Rhino Barn. The kids were quiet, hanging on her every word. It was exactly the kind of experience the Hubbards liked to support. Ted went back to Mike with a check for more than a million dollars to pay for that new barn.

Ashfall closed during construction. Two years later, the park reopened with a Rhino Barn that was eight times bigger than the original. It covered most of the area Mike originally wanted to include. More importantly, it meant researchers could keep working for many years to come.

Around that time, Ashfall was also named a National Natural Landmark. Not only was it a state park, but it was now recognized as a natural place unlike any other.

The area inside the new Rhino Barn is not yet fully explored. Interns dig carefully through untouched areas while visitors watch from the boardwalk. [Alison Pearce Stevens]

GHOST TRACKS

College interns from across the country and around the world continued to dig each summer. They uncovered more rhinos, camels, horses, and deer. The sheer number of skeletons buried in the ash astounded everyone who saw them—researchers and visitors alike. More rhino tracks emerged in places where interns excavated down to the sandy water-hole floor. There was lots of evidence of plant-eaters.

But what had happened to the predators?

A few bones of a dog the size of a fox (appropriately named the fox-sized dog) had been found in both the ash and the sand below. These were small dogs that wouldn't have been eating the large herbivores found in the ash bed. But *something* had been gnawing on the bones.

The year after the new Hubbard Rhino Barn opened, an entire dog skeleton appeared in the ash. This one was a raccoon-like dog: small, with a slender jaw and comb-like front teeth. Those funny **incisors** probably helped it hang onto slippery prey, like frogs and salamanders. It, too, was too small to have fed on the animals in the ash.

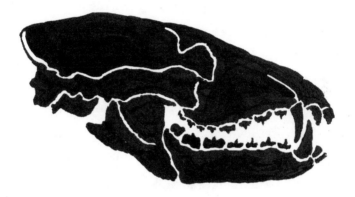

The skull of the raccoon-like dog.

The researchers knew from the sand below the ash that many different kinds of predators lived in the area at the time of the eruption, including bone-crushing dogs, bear-dogs, and *Barbourofelis*, the thin-sabered "cat." But the only signs the interns had seen of those animals were bones of plant-eaters that had been pulled away from the rest of the skeleton. Those bones usually had tooth marks on them.

Most of the skeletons were perfectly put together—every bone in its place. A few, however, had ribs or legs that had been moved around. Some ribs had been moved many feet from the rest of the skeleton. A few legs lay at awkward angles.

Those strange locations—plus the tooth marks on the bones—made it clear that scavengers had visited the water hole. Meat-eaters visited to eat the animals that had died there. Hunting might have been hard with ash blowing around and piling in drifts. Scavenging a growing pile of dead herbivores wasn't just easier—it probably kept those predators alive.

But which predators had been there? The most likely suspect: bone-crushing dogs. Those large dogs had strong jaws and a bony crest along the top of the skull where powerful jaw muscles once attached—powerful enough to break bone, or rip bones away from the rest of a dead animal. That, plus their long front legs (and shorter back ones), made them the hyenas of ancient Nebraska. Bones from bone-crushing dogs had been found in the sand, but the only signs researchers saw in the ash were scattered bones and tooth marks.

A predator known as a bone-crushing dog.

Then one recent summer, someone noticed something curious in the ash.

As interns scraped the ash away from ribs that had been discarded by scavengers, they left the ribs perched on a pedestal of ash. From the side of one of those pedestals, the ash looks striped. Layers of light gray ash are separated by thin white lines. Everyone assumed the horizontal lines were layers of ash that had settled into the water hole over time, and the color differences were simply variations in the ash itself.

That was true for some of the ash layers. But not all.

Geologist Jon Smith visited Ashfall as part of a project he was doing with Nebraska state geologist Matt Joeckel. When Jon first arrived, he climbed down into the ash bed, took one look at the ash column, and identified the thin white layers as fossil algae. No one else had thought twice about the white lines, but they turned out to hold important information.

Even though it was rapidly filling with ash, the water hole still held water. Algae grew on the surface, covering the ash. Then more rain and ash filled the pond, and more animals came, their large bodies causing the water to rise (like when you get into a bathtub). Algae again grew over sections of the ash. Again and again, layers of algae grew, eventually fossilizing and appearing as those thin white layers.

But what was really curious: In some spots (now that everyone was looking), the layers of algae looked like something had pushed down on them. They weren't horizontal like they were everywhere else.

Had something pushed down on the algae? Walked on it, perhaps? If so, that foot might have left a print behind.

The researchers carefully removed the ash above a layer of algae (called an **algal mat**) that had one of those indentations. As they oh so gently brushed the ash away from the top of the algal mat, circles appeared: a larger one with four smaller ones to one side. The central pad and four toes of a dog track.

It was a big one, too—a bone-crusher.

The right side of this image shows the brighter white of an algal mat, a layer of algae that formed on the surface of the water hole. [Alison Pearce Stevens]

At last, they had proof that the larger dogs had been in the ash bed at the time of the ashfall!

There was no telling how many ghostly tracks had been destroyed while digging for skeletons. Rick immediately had the interns change their approach to digging. They had to work much more slowly and carefully, dusting the ash off rather than scooping. Each time they reached an algal mat, they cleared it off from one end to the other. Not an easy task when the mats tore like tissue paper under their pointed tools.

Rick checked each and every algal mat after it was uncovered. Most of the time, there weren't any footprints, so he told the interns to keep digging. Those footprint-free algal mats had strange textures to them, though. Some had little dots, others had ripples, and still others high ridges.

But some algal mats were smooth and flat. These were the ones that usually had dog tracks. The weight of the dog as it padded across the drying algae would have pressed down on it, smoothing out any wrinkles.

When someone found a dog track, they marked it with a red plastic circle before continuing their search. Tracks soon appeared near many of the skeletons.

The dogs hadn't just visited once. They had come through time and again. The researchers knew this because they found tracks on many different layers at many different heights. The ones nearest the top came from the last dogs to visit. They probably didn't find much to eat, since the ash had begun covering the bodies below. Tracks closest to the sandy bottom had padded through first.

At the time this book was written, no bones of bone-crushing dogs had been uncovered in the ash. But with time, patience, and lots of digging that could change!

MORE EVIDENCE

Although the algal mats were an important discovery, Jon Smith and Matt Joeckel were actually interested in crystals. When Mike originally found the ash layer, he had searched—without success—for crystals to date the ash.

Even though they now had two types of evidence that put the age of Ashfall at almost twelve million years old, they wanted one more to be sure.

Remember that different kinds of radioactive elements decay at different rates. If several of those can be tested from the same location and all give the same age range, scientists can be confident about how old ash is.

When dating old rock, it's actually ash layers (not the rock itself) that are dated. That's because crystals form during a volcanic eruption. The eruption is kind of like hitting the start button on a stopwatch—it starts the clock. From that point on, radioactive decay causes one element to change into another. By calculating the amount of decay that has happened, scientists can figure out how long it's been happening. That tells them when the crystal burst out of the belly of a volcano.

Jon and Matt enlisted the help of geologist Andreas Möller and his student Eli Turner. They took samples from several layers of ash, including a darker band that lay just above the sandy bottom. This layer was where most of the diatoms and other microfossils had been found. Because no crystals had been found in the ash, people had thought for more than forty-five years that no crystals existed there.

Perhaps they just hadn't looked closely enough—or used the right techniques to separate the crystals from the ash.

Andreas and Eli took the samples back to Andreas's lab at the University of Kansas. There, they used chemical reactions to remove the glassy ash, then peered at what was left under a microscope. Lo and behold, they found what they were looking for: tiny crystals of zircon.

Zircon, which can be many different colors, is often used as a gemstone. But it also contains atoms of uranium. Uranium is a radioactive element that can be used to power nuclear power plants. Over time, it decays into lead. This process makes zircon crystals ideal for dating ash.

So that's what Andreas and Eli did. They tested each and

every one of those 136 crystals from the bottom of the ash and got a very clear answer. The crystals had shot out of the supervolcano 11.86 million years ago (plus or minus 130,000 years).

That matched the dates from both the fission tracks and the argon dating. Ashfall researchers could finally say with certainty that the eruption that created Ashfall happened almost twelve million years ago.

ALWAYS
SOMETHING NEW

It has now been fifty years since Mike stumbled upon the ash layer that opened up such extraordinary opportunities, not only for him, but for hundreds of students around the world. The ash held its secrets for millions of years, but it has slowly given them up to the paleontologists, geologists, and others who have worked there.

To date, more than 350 individual animals and 25,000 fossil bones and teeth have been found in, under, and around the water hole. A new ground-penetrating radar study successfully found fossils in the ash. Future excavation will focus on these areas, now that the paleontologists know where to dig. The GPR team also created a 3D digital map of the area inside the barn using a technique called LiDAR.

LiDAR is similar to radar but uses reflected light instead of sound.

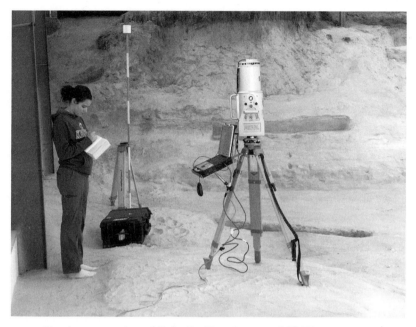

Graduate student Michelle Proulx uses LiDAR to create a 3D map of the area inside the Rhino Barn. [Rick Otto]

New species have been discovered. New scientific techniques have been developed, answering questions that have long remained mysteries.

Who knows what new techniques wait to be discovered. Or how they will uncover still more of the mystery behind Ashfall. It's a site that continues to surprise.

All it takes is the patient persistence of people who still love to dig in the dirt.

GLOSSARY

ALGAE: Simple, water-based plants that don't have stems or flowers. Some algae are tiny, with just a single cell. Other types are large plant-like seaweeds.

ALGAL MAT: A layer of algae that forms on top of water or wet rock.

ATMOSPHERE: The layer of air that surrounds our planet. The atmosphere is what allows us to breathe and helps trap the sun's heat, so that Earth isn't frozen all the time.

BEARDOG: An extinct animal that resembled both bears and dogs, but was neither. Some of these predators weighed more than four hundred pounds.

BROWSERS: Animals that eat leaves from shrubs and trees.

CALDERA: The crater left behind after a volcano erupts. Calderas often form when the eruption causes part of the volcano to collapse.

CANINES: Large, pointed teeth that are used to catch prey.

CARBON: Element number six, carbon is found in all living things. A carbon atom has six protons and six electrons.

CARTILAGE: Rubber-like support tissue found in the tip of the nose, outer ears, and other parts of the body.

CONVERGENT EVOLUTION: When two unrelated species evolve to have similar traits. Convergent evolution happens when they live in different, yet similar, places.

COORDINATES: Numbers that represent a site's exact location on the planet.

DECOMPOSE: To break down.

DENSE/DENSITY: How closely packed items are.

DIATOMS: Microscopic algae that make tiny glass houses.

ELECTRODES: Metal rods that conduct electricity.

ELECTRON: A negatively charged particle that orbits the center of an atom.

EROSION: Breakdown and removal of rock and soil by wind and water.

EVOLUTION: Change in a population of living organisms over time.

EXCAVATE: To carefully remove earth in order to find buried remains.

FISSION: The process in which the nucleus of an atom splits apart.

GEOLOGIST: A scientist who studies rocks and soils.

GPS: Global Positioning System. A network of devices, including smartphones, that receive signals from twenty-four satellites to know exactly where on Earth they are.

GRAZERS: Animals that eat grass.

GROUND-PENETRATING RADAR (GPR): Technology that sends high-frequency radio waves into the ground. These bounce back, showing where objects are located.

HOTSPOT: An area where plumes of super-hot magma push up against the underside of Earth's crust. When the magma pushes through, it creates a volcano.

HYOID: A horseshoe-shaped bone that attaches the tongue to the throat.

INCISORS: The front teeth, often used for biting.

INTERN: A person who does a job, usually for little (or no) money, to gain experience.

LATITUDE: How far north or south of the equator a place is located. Ranges from 0° (at the equator) to 90° (at the North or South Pole).

LONGITUDE: How far east or west of the prime meridian a place is located. Ranges from 0° (at the prime meridian in Greenwich, England) to 180° (on the opposite side of the planet).

MAGMA: Rock inside the earth that is so hot it's almost melted. Because it's not completely solid, currents can form.

MAMMAL: Warm-blooded animals that have fur and nurse their young.

MANTLE: Most of Earth's interior, made up of almost-solid rock. The mantle sits between the solid core and the outer crust.

MICROFOSSIL: A microscopic fossil.

OREODONT: A strange, plant-eating animal that used to be one of the most common mammals in North America. Now extinct, these medium dog–sized animals likely climbed trees to eat the leafy branches.

PALEOBOTANIST: A scientist who studies ancient plants by using fossil pollen, seeds, and other plant structures.

PALEONTOLOGIST: A scientist who studies ancient animal life, usually through fossils.

PETRIFIED: Turned to stone.

PHOTOSYNTHESIS: The process of making sugar from sunlight and carbon dioxide. Plants and algae, including diatoms, use this process to feed themselves. As a result, they produce oxygen that we breathe.

PLATE TECTONICS: The movement of Earth's crust.

RADIOACTIVE: Elements that lose parts of the atomic

nucleus over time, changing those atoms into a new chemical element.

RADIOACTIVE DECAY: The process of one element turning into another.

REPLICA: A copy of something.

RESPIRATORY SYSTEM: The parts of the body involved with breathing.

SAVANNA: A big, grassy plain with just a few trees.

SCANNING ELECTRON MICROSCOPE: Also called SEM, this microscope uses electrons to scan the outer surface of very small things.

SCAVENGE: To eat animals that are already dead.

SEDIMENT: Particles of soil, rock, or other matter that settle out in the bottom of a pond or other body of water.

SONAR: Sensing objects in the distance by bouncing sound waves off them.

SPECIMEN: Scientific term for an item collected from nature. This can be a fossil, a rock, or a living plant or animal.

SPORES: Protective, thick-walled structures that allow diatoms to survive harsh conditions.

SUPERVOLCANO: A volcano that shoots 240 cubic miles of lava, ash, and rock during a single explosive eruption.

TOPOGRAPHIC MAP: A map that shows the location and steepness of hills and valleys.

TRACHEA: A tube that connects lungs to the nose and mouth.

VERTEBRAE: Bones that make up the spine.

WATER HOLE: A pool of water in a generally dry area where animals go to drink. Water holes typically dry up during part of the year.

AUTHOR'S NOTE

Sometimes, life takes you in unexpected directions. This book would not have happened if I hadn't been invited to work at the University of Nebraska State Museum to help them create a whole new floor of exhibits telling the story of Nebraska through time. I learned about Ashfall, radioactive dating, horses, rhinos, crowned cranes, and much, much more. And I had the pleasure of working with many of the paleontologists who helped make Ashfall what it is today. Since I'm not originally from Nebraska, it was eye-opening for me to discover the natural treasures that— quite literally—lie beneath our feet. There is nowhere else in the world quite like Ashfall Fossil Beds State Park. If you happen to visit Nebraska or South Dakota, talk your parents into taking a detour to see it. You'll be glad you did.

RESOURCES

I consulted more than fifty sources and interviewed many scientists who work (or worked) at Ashfall. Here are some great sources if you're curious to learn more.

Ashfall Fossil Beds State Park
ashfall.unl.edu

How a Supervolcano Made the
Cenozoic's Coolest Fossils
youtube.com/watch?v=2ofNufZVcMU

Paleo Sleuths
paleosleuths.org/rhinos.html

ACKNOWLEDGMENTS

This book would not exist without the help of many people. First, thanks to Susan Weller and the education team at the University of Nebraska State Museum for bringing me on board and welcoming me with open arms. It was a pleasure to work with you all! Thanks to Mike Voorhies for inviting me into his home to reminisce about the early days of this project. *Huge* thanks to Rick Otto and Shane Tucker for answering email after email, meeting me in person to look at fossils and photos, taking photos for this book, and fact-checking the manuscript. Also to Mark Edlund and his students for letting me tag along on one of their field trips to Ashfall. And for letting me collect diatoms. (I'm still waiting to hear what you found in my sample!) Thanks to readers Kathy French, Nancy Sharp Wagner, Emily Timm, and Jenny

Heithoff for their feedback. Thanks to Angie Fox for her quick replies to my requests for image references. Matt Huynh, your artwork is phenomenal—thank you for illustrating this book! I'm grateful for the unexpected opportunity to share a bus ride with my wonderful editor, Laura Godwin, who fell in love with *Rhinos in Nebraska* by ride's end. To Rachel Murray, for her tireless enthusiasm. To my agent, Alexandra Weiss, for her constant support and critical feedback. And to Jeff, Cole, and Lane, who are my everything.

INDEX

Page numbers in *italics* refer to picture captions.